WYOMING'S OUTLAW DAYS

RICHARD PATTERSON

Johnson Books: Boulder

Cover photograph: Inner Circle of the "Wild Bunch."
(*Denver Public Library Western History Department*)

Map: Llyn French

ISBN: 0-933472-63-3

Printed in the United States of America by
Johnson Publishing Company
1880 South 57th Court
Boulder, Colorado 80301

CONTENTS

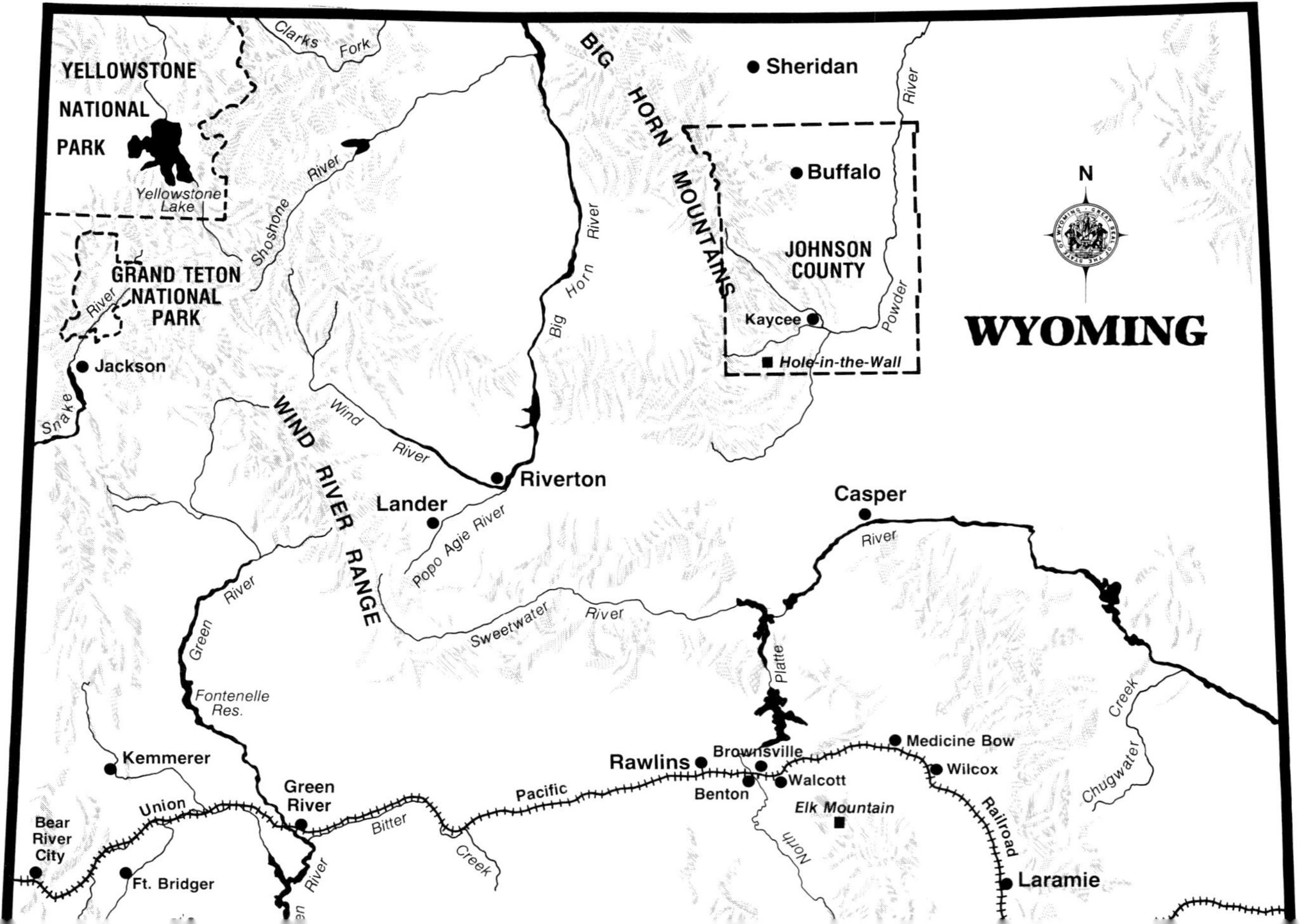
WYOMING
N
YELLOWSTONE NATIONAL PARK
Yellowstone Lake
GRAND TETON NATIONAL PARK
Clarks Fork
Shoshone River
Jackson
Snake River
BIG HORN MOUNTAINS
Big Horn River
Sheridan
Buffalo
JOHNSON COUNTY
Kaycee
Hole-in-the-Wall
Powder River
WIND RIVER RANGE
Wind River
Riverton
Lander
Popo Agie River
Casper
Platte River
North
Sweetwater River
Green River
Fontenelle Res.
Kemmerer
Bear River City
Ft. Bridger
Green River
Union Pacific Railroad
Bitter Creek
Rawlins
Brownsville
Benton
Walcott
Elk Mountain
Medicine Bow
Wilcox
Chugwater Creek
Laramie

THE RAILROAD TOWNS

As with much of the frontier, lawlessness came to Wyoming hand in hand with the railroad. Until survey crews began laying a route for the Union Pacific, there were few settlements in the territory; a half-dozen military forts, an assortment of stage stops, and a few clusters of homesteaders who built close together for protection from marauding Indians.

But with the coming of rails in the 1860s, a ribbon of "hell-on-wheels" towns sprung up across the southern half of the territory. The first town was Cheyenne, and the last was Evanston. Both survived, as did a dozen in between, mostly because they were chosen officially by the Union Pacific for inhabitation. Another dozen thrived for a while and then died, victims of the rails moving on.

For the short time they lived, these towns roared. The railroad filled men's pockets at quitting time, and the towns emptied them that night. Wherever the railroad paused, the tents and shacks would go up—mostly saloons and bed-down cribs—available for an hour or a night. If the settlement showed promise, peddler's wagons became general stores, bed-downs became boarding houses, and lawyers who never saw a law school hung out hastily painted land office signs. If the settlement showed real promise, a few dwellings were started, and maybe a meeting house was built.

Law and order was always slow in arriving at these hamlets, and when it did, it seldom caught up with a town already gone wild. A settlement might boast of a mayor or a sheriff, but these offices were often taken only for the graft that came with them. When justice was meted out, it was usually unofficial and came in the dead of night, courtesy of a few hardy citizens.

Located at the beginning of the rails, the town of Cheyenne suffered first at the hands of the outlaw element. But, to its advantage, the town was a division point for the railroad and thus prospered and grew rapidly. Also, unlike many of its sister settlements that would follow, Cheyenne was blessed early with an honest and courageous sheriff, Thomas Jefferson Carr.

Carr was elected in the fall of 1870 and wasted no time in cleaning up the town. The worst troublemaker at the time was the notorious Charlie Stanley, who ran a bawdy house in the Golden Gate district on Ferguson Street, which served as a "Robber's Roost" for local muggers and thieves. The sheriff and two deputies confronted Stanley on Ferguson Street, arrested him on an assortment of charges, and began to march him off to jail. But Carr, new on the job, had not done his homework. Stanley always carried a Derringer hidden in an inside pocket. Carr knew nothing of this, and Charlie promptly whipped out the gun and shot the sheriff in the ear. Carr, with blood spurting everywhere, wrenched the pistol away from his prisoner and slammed him up the side of the head with it. Now it was Charlie's turn to bleed. The blow served to clear Charlie's thinking, and he saw that he had little chance of escaping alive. He shrugged and with no more trouble allowed himself to be led to the lock-up.

The following month Sheriff Carr presided over the first legal execution in Wyoming Territory, the hanging of an "Indian half-breed" named John Boyer who had been convicted of killing two men at a roadhouse outside of town. Carr let it be known that the hanging was his official announcement that Cheyenne was a town outlaws had better avoid.

A favorite hideout for outlaws who preyed upon Cheyenne in the sixties was a ratty little encampment west of town that had sprung up during the building of the Union Pacific's magnificent Dale Creek Bridge. Work on the bridge, a wonder of its day because of its thousands of wooden girders, had hardly begun when mud-roofed shacks began sprouting up along the creek bed below. First used by construction workers and their families and then by a parade of camp followers, the settlement gradually became infested with riffraff from Cheyenne until, by the time the

Cheyenne, Wyoming Territory, in 1867. (*Wyoming State Archives, Museums and Historical Department*)

Thomas Jefferson Carr, courageous sheriff who brought law and order to Cheyenne in the early 1870s. (*Wyoming State Archives, Museums and Historical Department*)

Dale Creek Bridge. Work had hardly begun on the bridge when shacks began springing up along the creek bed below. The settlement became a favorite hideout for outlaws. (*Union Pacific Railroad Museum Collection*)

bridge was completed and the workers had left, few persons of orderly character could be found among the inhabitants.

In the sixties, prior to Sheriff Carr's arrival on the scene, what little law enforcement there was in Cheyenne was administered outside the law by vigilante groups. When word got around about the crowd out in Dale Creek, this was the first place the vigilantes headed with their ropes. After a few midnight lynchings, the Dale Creek rowdies got the message and moved on.

The next town of any consequence on the line was Laramie, and most of the Dale Creek scum settled there. Their antics soon became too much for Laramie's new mayor, lawyer M. C. Brown, and after only two months in office he threw up his hands and for all purposes turned the town over to the "robbers and garrotters." But the outlaw element's rule in Laramie was short-lived. Taking a tip from Cheyenne residents, Laramie's town fathers quickly formed vigilante committees and declared war on all miscreants.

Once in operation, the Laramie vigilantes surprised even themselves with their effectiveness. Not satisfied with cleaning up just within their own city limits, they roamed up

Benton, Wyoming Territory. Pen sketch of a busy night in "The Big Tent." Of all the railroad towns, Benton was perhaps the wildest. (*American Heritage Center, University of Wyoming*)

and down the line, giving notice to lawbreakers that merely moving on to the next town would not prove safe. As a result, the worst of the outlaw crowd leap-frogged the next half-dozen or so stops and came to rest in Brownsville, near the construction site of the Platte River bridge between Walcott and Rawlins.

Nourished by the thirsty bridge builders, the town of Brownsville blossomed quickly. Soon it could boast of a lawless element that rivaled the likes of the raunchy hell-holes of the Texas border country. With only token law enforcement and uninspired vigilante activity, Brownsville could easily have become Wyoming's prime example of the West gone wild. But its star faded abruptly; once the Platte River was spanned, the bridge builders moved on and took with them the reason for a town. The railroad had no interest in Brownsville, not even to the extent of a depot. Tents came down and shacks were dismantled, and the wood was thrown aboard wagons for the trip to the next settlement.

The next stop was Benton, just four miles down the line. This hamlet had even less to offer the railroad than

Brownsville, and its lifetime was equally as short. But while it flourished, some say it was even more turbulent than its neighbor up the tracks. In the summer of 1868, the *Cheyenne Leader*, commenting on Benton, reported that "there is more whiskey walking around in that community than any other of the same size in the world." And, according to Pence and Homsher's chronicle of Wyoming's bygone towns, "It was a rendezvous for outlaws, a hole-up for killers, a hurdy-gurdy for the madams. And for over one hundred who came to Benton, life ended without benefit of marker in the boothill." Not bad for a town that lasted just one summer and fall.

As towns like Brownsville and Benton flowered and faded, the outlaw element continued westward, picking up momentum as it went and descending en masse on whatever community the Union Pacific selected as its terminus for the winter of 1868-69. As October approached, it appeared that end-of-track would be somewhere just short of the Utah line, near Gilmer, a quaint log hamlet nestled quietly on the bank of Sulphur Creek in the vine-covered valley of the Bear River. Rumors ran up and down the railroad, but on October 13 speculation suddenly came to an end. Newspaper publisher Legh Freeman, in his track-following *Frontier Index*, ran this ad: "Wanted quick. Three good strong wagons and teams to transport the Frontier Index to Gilmer in Bear River Valley. Broad and high wagons and good strong sheets required."

The rush to the Bear River valley defies description. By the time Freeman found his wagons and loaded up his press and type case, the town of Gilmer, now renamed Bear River City, was sprouting close to 2,000 inhabitants: an assortment of fast-buck merchants, whiskey peddlers, land speculators, bunko artists, tinhorn gamblers, powdery prostitutes, general roughnecks, and a couple hundred honest citizens. What a few months earlier had been a quiet cluster of a half-dozen log and mud dwellings was now a twenty-four-hour town of tents and storefronts, bulging with the means to quench nearly every popular form of greed, lust, or thirst.

Bear River City, Wyoming Territory. As a result of violence the railroad by-passed the town as a winter terminus, and Benton became a ghost town. (*Wyoming State Archives, Museums and Historical Department*)

Although Freeman himself was a camp follower, he was all for decent communities along the U.P. tracks, so when Bear River City's criminal element began to show the upper hand, he used his newspaper to attack them fiercely. In early November he warned: "The gang of garroters who were recently driven away from some of our lower railroad towns are . . . congregating in our midst [and] had better go slow or they will find the place too hot for this location." His warning went unheeded, and soon no peaceful Bear River City resident could safely walk the streets after dark.

Probably at Freeman's urging, a vigilante committee was formed. Its first targets were three wild-eyed toughs from Montana who specialized in assaulting and robbing saloon customers. Justice was swift and sure. The scene was described by a local merchant, Alex Topence, who later chronicled the town's short history. "I got up one morning at my camp near the railroad track, and noticed something hanging near the railroad track, and I walked down to see what it was. It was those three fellows whom I knew had been banished from Montana in 1864. A tag was pinned to their coats, 'warning to the road agents.' "

But the vigilantes' choice of victims was unfortunate. One of the lynched cowboys had a brother working with the railroad construction gang camped at the edge of town. He stirred up some of the rough members of the outfit, and they stormed the town seeking revenge. They stopped off at one of the numerous Main Street saloons, however, and by the time they were ready to cause real trouble, they were too unsteady to accomplish much. A group of vigilantes quickly disarmed them and marched them off to jail.

With three of their comrades lynched and another handful sitting in jail, the crowd in the construction camp began to ferment. Generously fortified with whiskey and well armed with rifles, pickaxes, and torches, they eventually erupted into a mob and spilled out of camp into town. Their first stop was the jail, where they demanded the release of their friends. When the marshal refused, they promptly shot him, turned the prisoners loose, and set fire to the building. As they watched it burn, someone shouted, "Let's go after that damn editor!"

Legh Freeman, who slept in the same tent that housed his printing press, was unaware of the riot, but his neighbor, Alex Topence, heard the mob coming and alerted the editor. As the raging railroaders stormed into the tent from the front, Freeman raced out the back. Leaping on Topence's mule, which his neighbor had wisely saddled and bridled, the editor did not stop until he was safely out of town. On his way, he passed the town doctor, Frank Harrison, who later said Freeman was spurring his mule so fast "you could have played checkers on his flying coattail." Finding Freeman gone, the enraged mob smashed his press and set fire to his tent.

The railroaders were now entirely out of hand. The whiskey had worn off and had been replaced with utter madness. The next target was Nuckoll's general store, where a handful of townspeople had fled for safety. Fortified by Nuckoll's supply of guns and ammunition, the men in the group managed to fend off the attackers, preventing them from getting close enough to set the building ablaze.

The battle raged throughout the morning. Around noon, the townsmen managed to slip out a messenger to ride to nearby Fort Bridger for help. But by late afternoon, the mob began to tire of the seige and withdrew to the hills that overlooked the city, vowing to return during the night and set fire to the whole town. The townsmen posted guards at the end of the street, but the precaution was unnecessary. Filled with more whiskey, the mob finally slept off its rage. The troops from Fort Bridger arrived the following morning and declared martial law. The riot was over, and the citizens of Bear River City had their town back.

But the damage to the town was done. The Union Pacific wanted nothing to do with a community as obviously unstable as Bear River City. Moreover, a warm spell carried the tracklayers farther than expected, and the town missed out as the winter terminus. The railroad even refused to put a switch on its line at the town, and Bear River City soon died.

In less than a year the railroad had swept through the territory. The new towns that survived fostered early visions of statehood. In October 1869, the *Cheyenne Leader* was even boosting that city as a natural choice for a new site for the nation's capital, citing its central location, attractive climate and excellent transportation facilities. But despite the railroad, the entire territory still had only 8,104 residents. Wyoming was far from being ready to settle down. Law and order had yet to replace the vigilante's noose. The territory was still young, and Wyoming's violent years had just begun.

THE HOLE-IN-THE-WALL

The Hole-in-the-Wall itself is unremarkable; yet, just the sound of the name brings visions of Butch Cassidy, the Sundance Kid, and the hordes of renegades who prowled Wyoming's Powder River range. In fact, you cannot even call it a "hole." It is more of a notch, roughly V-shaped, near the rim of the "Red Wall," a steep vermillion cliff in southwestern Johnson County. To reach it you must climb a narrow, winding, rock-strewn game trail.

The Hole is mentioned today on most Wyoming highway maps. It lies about 16 miles southwest (as the crow flies) of Kaycee, a tiny Johnson County town of 275 hearty inhabitants on Interstate 25, about 50 miles south of Buffalo. The nearest public road to the Hole is County Road 190, which follows the upstream path of the narrow valley of the Wind River's Middle Fork as it rises gently west out of Kaycee toward the stately Big Horn Mountains. About 12 miles out, Road 190 begins to wind west, then slightly north, and finally leaves the river to follow Beaver Creek up to the remains of Gus Barnum's ancient post office, a dirt-roofed, stone-floored relic of Johnson County's wilder days.

If you leave the road where it leaves the river, and follow the Powder's Middle Fork south to where it loses itself in the beginnings of the Big Horn's rolling foothills, you will eventually come to one of the river's major tributaries, Buffalo Creek, still called by old-timers the South Fork of the Powder. Here the landscape suddenly gets lonelier and wilder. Far to the east you see emerging an ominous red sandstone cliff, to which the creek seems mysteriously drawn in wide, jagged swaths.

Against the wall the stream twists and turns, as if unsure of its path, and finally begins to edge eastward. Seeking, darting, the waters leave the cliff, return to it, leave again, and then, as if beckoned by the stern mountains, start a long, sweeping arc westward toward the Big Horns. At the beginning of this turn, if you look hard to your left and scan the wall carefully, you can see it. You are at the legendary Hole.

Tales about the Hole-in-the-Wall are endless and over the years have crisscrossed the frontier with the same embellishments lavished upon the stories of the outlaws who made it famous. One of the most popular tales, one that has been told and retold until it has become fused into Hollywood westerns, is that behind the Hole once lay a classic outlaw town, replete with false-front store buildings, houses with picket fences, and raggedy children running about, all pro-

Break in Johnson County's steep vermillion cliffs leading to the famous Hole-in-the-Wall. When outlaw gangs eluded posses in the area, it was assumed that there was a "hole" through which they escaped to the valley on the opposite side. There was no hole, but rather a hidden trail leading to a notch at the top. (*American Heritage Center, University of Wyoming*)

tected by towering cliffs through which there was but one narrow entrance, guarded day and night by sharpshooters with Winchesters.

True, there is a valley behind the wall, and once there were even rough-hewn cabins here and there, but nothing resembling a town, and nothing quite so impregnable. In fact, few persons familiar with the area during the outlaw days could agree on just how valuable it was as a hideout, except perhaps that a posse approaching directly from the east could be held off fairly easily. (Butch Cassidy was supposed to have said that twelve men could stand off a hundred at the Hole's entrance.) But the ability to defend the valley at the notch in the Red Wall meant little, because anybody familiar with the valley would not attack from that direction. To the north, west, and south there were great rolling foothills, all of which contained passable trails. Years earlier Indian hunters traveled in and out of the valley by these and other routes, as their traces still show, especially in the grassy meadows of the Powder River's Middle Fork. Old timers can tell you about the great Sioux Trail, which crosses the valley from north to south and eventually winds its way through the entire length of Johnson County.

Although the Hole-in-the-Wall valley was not impregnable, it was indeed secluded and thus offered an ideal haven for outlaws. Thelma Gatchill Condit, local historian, who spent nearly a lifetime exploring the region, suggests why:

> It was the one place, because of its wild bigness and rugged terrain, ideally safe and delightfully isolated, full of little grassy mountain pockets where tired, used horses, as well as pilfered broncs, could graze contentedly until moving-on time; full of little hidden canyons especially made for the leisurely changing of brands. It was not a hurry-up place at all; there was always plenty of *safe* time. Here train robbers could be swallowed up like magic, bringing sheriffs' posses to a sudden halt, leaving them feeling furiously foolish to have been foiled so completely and unexpectedly when the moment of closing-in seemed so certain.

Condit also believed that the Hole-in-the-Wall valley was popular with the outlaws because it was an ideal training ground for their horses. Butch Cassidy in particular was obsessed with the idea that a bandit's fate rested with the quality of his mount. Before he became a familiar face on wanted posters, Cassidy owned a ranch in the valley, on Blue Creek, about 10 miles northwest of the Hole. It was said that Cassidy's corrals frequently held some of the best horseflesh in the West; on a given day one might find a magnificent mixture of Morgan, Thoroughbred, Arabian, Palomino, and American, all in training over the valley's slippery shale ledges, high cutbanks, and steep foothills.

In addition, the Hole-in-the-Wall valley was a safe harbor for thieves because of the attitude of the permanent residents there. They were not inquisitive. Honest homesteaders and ranchers in the valley—and there were a handful—did not ask questions of others who might not be so honest. The feeling was that what a man did elsewhere was his own business as long as he behaved himself in the valley.

The outlaw crowd usually did behave themselves behind the wall. For amusement, however, they occasionally plagued neighboring towns, especially Anderson (now Thermopolis) over in Hot Springs County, where one day in the early nineties Butch Cassidy, in a rare fit of intoxication or anger, shot up the town's cafe, and Harry Longabaugh (the Sundance Kid) did the same to the saloon.

For general carousing, the boys from the Hole had two favorite haunts. One was the saloon at nearby Kaycee, then just a crossroads, owned by two men named Tom O'Day and John Nolan, both of whom were said to be part-time rustlers or outside "contact men." O'Day's job, the story went, was to ride into a cow camp or ranch on the pretext of just "passing through" and to "spot the herd," that is, gather up the lay of the land and the strength of the defenses—information his comrades would later need when they came calling at midnight.

A willow grove near the Hole-in-the-Wall into which outlaws would disappear when being chased by posses. (*American Heritage Center, University of Wyoming*)

The other hang-out for the Hole-in-the-Wall bunch was Buffalo's Zindel Saloon, which in later years became the Rainbow Cafe, a favorite stop for tourists.

No one knows for sure who first used the Hole-in-the-Wall to hide from the law. Some say it was a rustler named Sanford "Sang" Thompson, who discovered in the mid-eighties that by shifting a few boulders about on the trail leading up to the notch at the wall's rim, one could make it appear that there was no trail at all. There were those who will tell you that Thompson and his comrades became so successful with their deception that they could drive stolen cattle up the trail and over the rim to a concealed makeshift corral on the other side and leave pursuing stock detectives scratching their heads in amazement. Some day that is how the Hole got its name. Thinking the wall could not be climbed, the pursuers concluded that there had to be a tunnel somewhere.

Other stories suggest that the Hole was used by renegades long before Thompson's day. In any case, the Hole-in-the-Wall country was under the control of outlaws off and on for fifteen to twenty years. As a common hideout, it finally fell into disuse following the Wild Bunch's last major holdup, the robbery of the Great Northern Coast Flyer at Exeter, Montana, in July 1901. The gang broke up after that, and without these renegades around, the region gradually became attractive to honest homesteaders who soon outnumbered their less-savory predecessors.

THE JAMES BOYS IN WYOMING

It is not widely known, but Missouri bank and train robber Frank James, and perhaps the notorious Jesse James himself, rode the outlaw trail in Wyoming.

It was in the spring of 1878, two years after the James brothers' narrow escape in a bank robbery attempt at Northfield, Minnesota. Still on the run, Frank drifted west, into the Powder River region of northern Wyoming. Prowling the area at the time was a local rustler named Big Nose George Parrott who led a makeshift gang of former road agents from the Black Hills region of the Dakotas.

How James and Parrott met is not known, but it is not too surprising that they decided to join forces. Frank was staying out of Missouri until things cooled down there, and undoubtedly the Powder River area seemed a good place to lie low for a while. Still, he would need money now and then, and he wanted to keep his hand in. He was an outlaw by profession, an art at which one could become rusty from too much time off.

Big Nose George Parrott, on the other hand, was still a novice. He had achieved an early reputation as a bad sort, but as an outlaw he was still considered small time. To ride with Frank James would be an honor. Frank needed someone like Parrott, or at least Parrott's gang. It would have been too risky for James to try to put together an outfit. Parrott could supply one ready-made—if not efficient, at least experienced, and apparently trustworthy.

Frank James reportedly rode under the name McKinney and for the most part stayed in the background, content to let Parrottt act as leader. It is believed, however, that Frank was the moving force behind the outfit, as the gang prepared to graduate from small-time holdups to big-time robbery. (There is some speculation—but little proof—that brother Jesse also took an assumed name and rode along.)

Frank was adept at robbing both banks and trains. There were few banks in the territory at the time, so the natural choice was a Union Pacific express car. In early June, they selected as their first victim the U.P.'s Westbound Express No. 3, at a site near Carbon, now a caved-in ghost town on the sun-blistered plains between the present towns of Medicine Bow and Rawlins.

As a pioneer in the art of train robbery, Frank had experimented with several methods of bringing a locomotive to a halt in order to gain access to the express car. His favorite method was the simplest—wreck it. He usually accomplished this by dislodging a rail. The fact that many

Frank James. (*Kansas State Historical Society, Topeka*)

lives could be lost as a result of such handiwork never seemed to enter Frank's mind. He wanted the treasures the express cars held, and he usually went about getting at them the quickest way possible.

Breaking into the section toolhouse for picks and shovels was easy, and in minutes the Parrott gang, with Frank supervising, had pried loose a rail on the U.P. track just outside of Carbon. But as they were wrapping a wire around the rails, in order to yank it aside as the train approached, they heard the sound of a handcar coming down the track from the opposite direction. Scrambling for cover in the tall sagebrush, they barely made it out of sight as John Brown, a crusty U.P. section foreman, came pumping by. Like any track worker worth his salt, he had a keen eye for trouble along the line, and he immediately spotted the disjointed rail. Brown was no fool: he knew the westbound was due any moment, and he realized that whoever loosened the rail was likely to be hiding nearby. Without a sideways glance, the quick-witted foreman kept pumping away as if nothing was wrong.

Later, Big Nose George Parrott was to say that Frank James wanted to put a bullet in Brown's back before he got out of sight. Parrott claimed that he stopped James, thinking that Brown had missed seeing the loose rail and not wanting to alert anyone else in the area with a gunshot. Foreman Brown, of course, sped down the track and flagged the oncoming express. When the train did not appear, Parrott realized his mistake and probably caught all kinds of hell from Frank. The Parrott gang's first try at big-time robbery was a flop.

But the gang's troubles were just beginning. When word of the incident was sent out along the line, posses were quickly formed at both Laramie and Rawlins and were soon converging on the scene.

By the time the authorities arrived, the outlaws' trail was cold, so the posses formed two groups and headed in the two directions the fugitives were most likely to take: north along the Medicine Bow River and west toward the town of Hanna.

Two of the possemen, Henry "Tip" Vincent, a U.P. detective, and Bob Widdowfield, a coal mine boss from Carbon, had a hunch the outlaws might have fled south toward Elk Mountain. After a while, Vincent and Widdowfield did pick up what appeared to be tracks leading toward Rattlesnake Pass. Unwisely, they followed the tracks right in, never dreaming the outlaws would be waiting. A bullet from Big Nose Parrott's rifle split Widdowfield's skull. Vincent spurred his horse and made a run for it, but he got less than a hundred yards. Their bodies were found several days later, partially hidden in brush near the foot of Elk Mountain, stripped of clothing and valuables. Officials of Widdowfield's company vowed to his bereaved wife that they would "right the wrong" done to her husband, and they promised to erect a monument in his name.

Following the killings, the Parrott gang split up and headed for parts unknown. Later that fall, Frank James showed up in southwestern Wyoming at a ranch called the Circle K, near Bitter Creek, where he was soon joined by Jesse. The authorities were still looking for the two back in Missouri, and now, with Wyoming lawmen on their trail as well, the Bitter Creek region seemed a good place to spend the winter. As it turned out, their decision almost put an end to the famous brothers.

The two Missouri renegades knew little about the dangers of late winter blizzards in the Flaming Gorge country. In March 1879, while staying at a cabin on Henry's Fork, Frank and Jesse set out on foot to retrieve their horses, which had broken loose in search of food. Caught far from the cabin in a sudden storm, they were soon hopelessly lost in the blowing snow. A local man named Jim Baker was along, and he probably had warned the two about the weather, but Frank and Jesse James were not prone to listen to the advice of others. They had enough sense to stay along the bank of the creek, but before long they were drenched from falling into the icy water. As the story was later told, they came within minutes of freezing to death before they stumbled across another cabin.

Having had enough of Wyoming's harsh weather, the two outlaws headed south the following month, leaving dozens of proud residents of the Flaming Gorge country with stories to tell of crossing paths with the famous James brothers.

Frank's partners in the aborted train robbery affair did not fare as well. Dutch Charley Burris, who was thought to have shot Tip Vincent at Rattlesnake Pass, was captured a short time later in Montana and returned to Wyoming by train. When the train stopped at Carbon, he was dragged out of the coach and into the depot by an angry mob. Surrounded by friends of the dead Bob Widdowfield, Dutch Charley figured his only hope was to confess and plead for mercy. A Union Pacific telegrapher was summoned, and he took down the outlaw's confession. But instead of being taken to jail, as Charley had expected, he was marched outside and made to stand on a barrel. A rope was quickly placed around his neck, and the other end thrown over a telegraph pole. Someone asked the outlaw if he had anything to say before he met his maker. But before he could answer, Bob Widdowfield's widow stepped out from the crowd. "No, the son-of-a-bitch has nothing to say," and she kicked the barrel out from under him.

Big Nose George Parrott was arrested the following year, also in Montana. He lived longer than Dutch Charley, but not much. Shortly after being locked up in the Rawlins jail, he too gave a confession, thinking it might save his life. He was promptly dragged outside and, like Charley, left dangling from a telegraph pole.

THE KILLING OF NATE CHAMPION

The Hole-in-the-Wall country had its desperados, some as mean and ornery as could be found on the frontier, but the most common crime along the powder River was rustling steers. And to many a homesteader in the region, stealing a steer was not all that serious an offense, especially if it was from one of the large cattle outfits, for whom most Johnson County residents had little fondness.

In the late 1880s, the Powder River rustlers were led by a dashing ex-Texan named Nate Champion. Nate's riders were expert and colorful. A favorite tale still told around Buffalo and Casper is that the gang, under the guise of a local "stockowners' association," eventually became so powerful that it would set its own "round-up date," which it would announce by nailing up posters on telegraph poles.

Many members of Butch Cassidy's Wild Bunch of the 1890s got their start riding with Champion's rustlers, including the Logan brothers, Flat Nose George Currie, and Tom O'Day.

But that is only one side of the story. Nate Champion, some would argue, may have rustled a few steers, but on the whole he was not a bad sort. In fact, to many Powder River residents of the day, he was a hero, and when his end finally came, he is remembered for dying a hero's death. To Sam T. Clover, a reporter for the *Chicago Herald* who covered the cattlemen's war with the rustlers in the early nineties, Nate Champion was indeed "the bravest man in Johnson County."

The year was 1892. Infuriated by the brazenness of Champion and his followers, the Wyoming Stock Growers' Association decided to put an end, once and for all to rustling in the Powder River region. Quietly, the cattlemen began soliciting funds for a war chest. The figures vary, but some say each member was assessed $1,000 until a total of $100,000 was raised. With the first money collected, the cattlemen hired a former Texas peace officer, Tom Smith, to ride down to the Lone Star State and round up an army of adventurers who would be willing, for a price, to wage battle with the cattle thieves of Johnson County. The pay was to be five dollars a day plus expenses, a $3,000 accident insurance policy, and, according to some reports, a bonus of $50 for each rustler killed. Although most of the volunteers recruited were a hard-nosed lot, some balked at the idea of hired killing until Smith assured them that the men they were to pursue were despicable outlaws who sorely needed thinning out.

While Smith was marshaling the Texas contingent, the cattlemen back home were gathering volunteers from Wyoming and neighboring states, mostly former peace officers and part-time hired guns who drifted in and out of this kind of work.

On April 8, 1892, the cattlemen's army of invaders, which numbered just over fifty, set up camp outside Casper, thinly disguised as a crew of railroad surveyors. Tucked in the pocket of Frank Canton, former Texas outlaw and commander of the Wyoming section of the brigade, was a "dead list," names of suspected rustlers marked for elimination. Prominent on the list was, of course, the name of Nate Champion.

The invaders did not have long to wait. Word came that Champion and a fellow cow thief, Nick Ray, were holed-up in a cabin on the K-C Ranch, about 15 miles northeast of the Hole-in-the-Wall. The "regulators," as the group preferred to call itself, arrived at the ranch near dawn and quietly surrounded the cabin, a tumble-down log and frame shack once used for a line camp. Champion and Ray had had two visitors during the night, an old trapper and his partner. These two awoke first and went outside to wash in the creek. They were quickly overpowered and whisked away into the nearby woods. A few minutes later Ray appeared. The regulators, now eager for a kill, opened fire as soon as he stepped into the open. Although mortally wounded, he managed to crawl back to the cabin door, where Champion, with his gun blazing, reached out and dragged him inside.

It was now daylight, and Champion could see clearly the size of the force that surrounded him. Yet he continued to fight on, refusing to acknowledge shouts from Canton and others to surrender and throw out his weapons. "Champion was shooting out of the portholes as fast as he could burn ammunition," Canton later said. "He was an expert shot with a rifle and came near getting several of our men."

Guns blazed for three hours, then the attackers suddenly stopped firing. Inside, huddled beneath a window, Cham-

Kaycee, Wyoming, at the turn of the century. The nearest town to the famous Hole-in-the-Wall, it was also here, at the nearby Kaycee Ranch, that the Johnson County War started. (*Wyoming State Archives, Museums and Historical Department*)

pion was pretty sure he knew why. He had heard the sounds of hatchets chopping away at dry wood and brush—they were going to burn him out!

By late afternoon a large pile of kindling lay on a makeshift wagon which had been wheeled against the north wall of the cabin. A torch was readied, lighted, and thrown onto the pile. Reporter Sam Clover, who had followed the regulators out from Casper, described the scene.

> The roof of the cabin was the first to catch on fire, spreading rapidly downward until the north wall was a sheet of flames. Volumes of smoke poured in at the open window from the burning wagon, and in a short time through the plastered cracks of the log house puffs of smoke worked outward. Still the doomed man remained doggedly concealed, refusing to reward them by his appearance. The cordon of sharpshooters stood ready to fire upon him the instant he started to run. Fiercer and hotter grew the flames, leaping with mad

impetuosity from room to room until every part of the house was ablaze and only the dugout at the west end remained intact.

"Reckon the cuss has shot himself," remarked one of the waiting marksmen. "No fellow could stay in that hole a minute and be alive."

These words were barely spoken when there was a shout, "There he goes!" and a man clad in his stocking feet, bearing a Winchester in his hands and a revolver in his belt, emerged from a volume of black smoke that issued from the rear door of the house and started off across the open space surrounding the cabin into a ravine, fifty yards south of the house, but the poor devil jumped square into the arms of two of the best shots in the outfit, who stood with leveled Winchesters around the bend waiting for his appearance. Champion saw them too late, for he overshot his mark just as a bullet struck his rifle arm, causing the gun to fall from his nerveless grasp. Before he could draw his revolver a second shot struck him in the breast and a third and fourth found their way to his heart.

Nate Champion, the king of cattle thieves, and the bravest man in Johnson County, was dead. Prone upon his back, with his teeth clenched and a look of mingled defiance and determination on his face to the last, the intrepid rustler met his fate without a groan and paid the penalty of his crimes with his life. A card bearing the significant legend, "Cattle thieves, beware!" was pinned to his blood soaked vest, and there in the dawn, with his red sash tied around him and his half-closed eyes raised toward the blue sky, this brave but misguided man was left to die by the band of regulators who, having succeeded in their object, rapidly withdrew from the scene of the double tragedy.

But before they left, several members of the raiders searched through the dead man's pockets. There they found a small notebook, a pocket memorandum, soaked with blood and partially shattered by a bullet. Inside, in Champion's handwriting, was an entry bearing the day's date, April 9, 1892. Following this were the words:

> Me and Nick was getting breakfast when the attack took place. Two men here with us—Bill Jones and another man. The old man went after water and did not come back. His friend went out to see what was the matter and he did not come back. Nick is shot, but not dead yet. He is awful sick. I must go and wait on him. It is now about two hours since the first shot. Nick is still alive; they are still shooting and are all around the house. Boys, there is bullets coming in like hail. Them fellows is in such shape I can't get at them. They are shooting from the stable and river and back of the house Nick is dead, he died about 9 o'clock. I see a smoke down at the stable. I think they have fired it. I don't think they intend to let me get away this time.
>
> It is now about noon. There is someone at the stable yet; they are throwing a rope out at the door and drawing it back. I guess it is to draw me out. I wish that duck would get further so I could get a shot at him. Boys, I don't know what they have done with them two fellows that staid last night. Boys, I feel pretty lonesome just now. I wish there was someone here with me so we could watch all sides at once. They may fool around until I get a good shot before they leave. It's about 3 o'clock now. There was a man in a buckboard and one on horseback just passed. They fired on them as they went by. I don't know if they killed them or not. I seen lots of men come out on horses on the other side of the river and take after them. I shot at the men in the stable just now; don't know if I got any or not. I must go and look out again. It don't look as if there is much show of my getting away. I see twelve or fifteen men. One looks like (name is scratched out). I don't know whether it is or not. I hope they did not catch them fellows that run over the bridge towards Smith's. They are shooting

at the house now. If I had a pair of glasses I believe I would know some of those men. They are coming back. I've got to look out.

Well, they have just got through shelling the house like hail. I heard them splitting wood. I guess they are going to fire the house to-night. I think I will make a break when night comes, if alive. Shooting again. I think they will fire the house this time. It's not night yet. The house is all fired. Goodbye, boys, if I never see you again.

Nathan D. Champion

BRINGING IN TETON JACKSON

Up in Death Canyon, not far from the site of the old J. Y. Dude Ranch on Phelps Lake, there is a tiny green meadow beside a deep, narrow mountain stream. It is said that if you go to that meadow, get down on your hands and knees, and carefully part the fragile blue harebell and pale, elegant Columbine, you can still see the weathered remains of a 100-year-old drift fence, once said to house stolen ponies, cautiously secreted away from prowling vigilantes who frequently combed the Snake River Valley below.

Although never as famous as the other "holes" so often connected with Wyoming outlaws—the legendary notch in Johnson County's magnificent Red Wall, for example, or the desolate Brown's Hole that straddles the Utah line—western Wyoming's lush Jackson Hole was at one time a popular hideaway for thieves and cutthroats who roamed the giant Teton range. Butch Cassidy spent much of his leisure time there, and he was said to have stashed part of the loot from one of his robberies somewhere along the willowy banks of Cache Creek.

Jackson Hole, the name given to the valley along the Snake River running from the town of Jackson northward to the northern edge of what is now Grand Teton National

Park, was indeed once an outlaw's paradise. One observer described the rugged wilderness in these terms:

> Every entrance lay through intricate solitudes. The Snake River came in . . . through canyons and mournful pines and marshes to the north, and went out the south between formidable chasms. Every tributary . . . rose among high peaks and ridges, and descended into the valley by well-nigh impenetrable courses: Pacific Creek from Two Ocean Pass, Buffalo Fork from no pass at all. Black Rock from To-we-ge-tee Pass—all of these, and many more, were the waters of loneliness, among whose thousand hiding places it was easy to get lost.

But despite the natural sanctuary offered by the valley, the area never became a true outlaw stronghold as did the Hole-in-the-Wall and Brown's Hole. Generally, the Teton

Jackson, Wyoming. The wilderness in the distance became a popular hideaway for thieves and cutthroats who roamed the Teton range. *(American Heritage Center, Universtiy of Wyoming)*

contingent of hell raisers did their hell raising elsewhere and slipped in and out of the valley virtually unnoticed. Outlaws did venture into the town of Jackson from time to time, for supplies and an evening's entertainment, and occasionally found the law waiting for them there, but if there were any spectacular shootouts between the good guys and bad guys (as presently acted out on summer nights for the tourist crowd), they have been lost to history.

Lawbreakers came and went without causing much trouble in Jackson, and thus for the most part they were left alone by the locals. It was said that the residents of Jackson Hole distrusted the law and courts, and when a troublemaker occasionally did go too far, he was taken care of privately, with no interference from the outside. This practice was said to have stemmed from an incident early in the town's history, when a drifter accused of a grisly murder was sent down to Evanston for hanging, but, thanks to a sharp-tongued lawyer, came back a free man.

Aside from Butch Cassidy, the most famous outlaw to roam the Jackson Hole region was probably a notorious gunman and horse thief named Harvey Gleason, who preferred to ride under the name Teton Jackson. Teton was downright mean and could be counted on to cause trouble of some kind wherever he went. A big man, well over six feet, with rawbone features, flaming red hair, and "eyes as black as a snake's." Jackson was the sort of outlaw that every local sheriff was supposed to be looking for, but few wanted to find.

Little is known of Jackson's early years, except that he ran a mule train for the army during the Sioux War. Apparently he became dissatisfied with government pay and decided to sell a few of the army's mules on his own. For this he ended up in the guard house, from which he promptly escaped by killing two troopers. He fled to the Tetons, took his new name, and joined up with a gang of renegades calling themselves the "Destroying Angels." Their specialty was raiding ranches and homesteads along the Utah and Idaho borders.

By the early 1880s, Teton had added two more names to

his list of murder victims, both United States deputy marshals who unwisely tried to trail him into his mountain lair. The Territory of Utah placed a $3,500 reward on Jackson's head, but there were few attempts to collect it, since it generally meant following the same path the dead lawmen had taken.

Around 1883, Jackson and his gang began concentrating on cutting horses out of well-stocked herds in Idaho, Utah, and Oregon. They would gather up ten or twelve at a time, stash them away in temporary corrals until they had fifty or so, then drive them east into one of Jackson Hole's hidden meadows. There, after changing brands where necessary, the gang would split into groups of three and four, and each take a small bunch north along the Snake River and then east toward the Big Horns and Johnson county. From there, they would work their way along the stage routes to the mining area around Deadwood, where good horses brought hefty prices.

Jackson and his band profited handsomely from their operation for several years. Then one day in 1885, the sheriff at Blackfoot, Idaho, received a tip that several horses stolen from ranches in his vicinity had been seen with a small herd being driven toward the Big Horn basin. He immediately wired the office of Frank Canton, sheriff of Johnson County, in Buffalo. From the description given by witnesses, Canton and the Idaho sheriff were pretty certain the man driving the herd was Teton Jackson. And Canton, after studying the problem for a few mintues, came up with a good idea where Jackson might be intercepted.

Near Paint Rock Creek Canyon in the Big Horn basin there was an isolated cabin belonging to an old trapper whom Canton for some time had suspected of being in league with horse thieves. If Jackson was headed for that area, it was a good bet he would be staying at least one night at that cabin. Canton quickly located on a map the spot where Jackson and his horses had last been seen and calculated the time it would take him to reach the cabin. He concluded that Teton would likely arrive that very night. He

Frank Canton. As sheriff of Johnson County, he captured the notorious Teton Jackson and in 1892 rode with the "Regulators" in the Johnson County War. (*American Heritage Center, University of Wyoming*)

also concluded that if he left Buffalo immediately, and rode hard, he could reach the cabin before morning.

Canton selected his best two deputies and they left at once. Ten hours later they were camped in woods not far from the old trapper's cabin, their Winchesters trained on the door. Just before dawn, they saw a candle being lighted inside; then, a few minutes later sparks coming from the chimney. Whoever was inside would be warming himself before the fire: it would be a good time to make a move.

Canton, with his men covering him, cautiously sneaked up to the door and peeked through a crack. In the dim light he saw a man he recognized as Jackson squatting before the fire trying to light his pipe. He was only partially dressed, and he had not yet buckled on his six-gun, which was lying on the floor just within reach.

"Throw up your hands!" Canton shouted, as he called for his deputies to bring the handcuffs. With his prisoner in cuffs, Canton sent his deputies out to see about rounding up the stolen horses. Canton and Jackson were now alone in the cabin, sitting about six feet apart. Jackson's black eyes burned, furious at being caught so easily. The sheriff sized up the outlaw who sat before him. If the many stories about the man were true, it was going to be a long trip back to Buffalo.

"The handcuffs are too tight," Jackson mumbled. "The blood won't circulate. If you take 'em off, I'll keep quiet and promise not to hurt you."

Canton smiled. "I'm not a bit uneasy about you hurting me. I got no objections to taking them off. You're the one taking all the chances. If I take them off, and you make the slightest move, I'll kill you." The outlaw nodded, and the sheriff threw him the keys.

Once free of the cuffs, Jackson rubbed his wrists and squinted at the fire. Neither man spoke. Finally, the outlaw grunted and turned to face the lawman. "You'll never take me to Buffalo, sheriff. I'm putting you on notice right now. I'm a better man than you, even with that six-shooter you got there."

"Jackson," Canton replied, "I'm taking you to Buffalo. It'll be either dead or alive. Fact is, I'd rather take you dead, since you'd be a lot less trouble." Then he picked up the handcuffs and tossed them back to the outlaw. "If you don't get these back on in ten seconds, you're gonna take your medicine right here." Jackson put the cuffs back on, but the sheriff suddenly got the feeling that his trouble was just beginning.

When they saddled up, Canton instructed his deputies to

tie Jackson's feet together underneath his horse's belly. He expected the outlaw to raise a fuss. It was a dangerous way to ride. If the horse stumbled and threw his rider, he could be kicked to death in seconds. But Jackson did not say a word. This worried Canton. He could not help but wonder if the outlaw's friends were at that very moment watching them from the same woods he and his deputies had hidden in that morning. Jackson had told the sheriff that he had sent his two gang members back to Jackson Hole the day before, but Canton did not believe him. One man would not have tried to maneuver fifty horses through the mountains.

But once they were under way, Canton breathed easier. If Jackson's boys were around, they would surely have jumped them immediately. It was more likely that they were off on an errand. It was now a matter of getting a good lead on them before they returned and figured out what had happened.

A steady rain began to fall. Damn, thought Canton, a blind man could follow their tracks in the mud.

All went well until just before they reached the top of the pass out of the mountains. Ahead on the trail the rain had turned about twenty feet of their narrow path into a mushy bog—about a half-foot of sod and the rest pure hoof-sucking mud, the kind a horse can get into and never get out of. Canton sized up the situation and then ordered his deputies to start across, single file. The turf was stronger than it looked: once-dry prairie grass that had become thick and spidery with recent heavy rains. The deputies made it, and then Jackson, carefully guiding his horse around the tracks of his predecessors, reached solid ground on the far side. Now it was Canton's turn. Slowly he eased his mount forward, confident now that the sod would hold. It didn't.

As his horse broke through, Canton went head first into the mud. The horse, struggling for its life, found its footing and bounded on, leaving the enraged sheriff floundering in the mire. Once under way, Canton's horse dashed for the nearest solid ground, which happened to be right next to where Jackson sat on his mount. The outlaw, meanwhile, was thoroughly enjoying the sheriff's plight. But as he roared with laughter, Jackson began easing his horse around, ever so slowly, so that he was directly between the sheriff's horse and the two deputies, a dozen yards ahead on the trail. Still laughing, he leaned to the side, and, as if to calm the sheriff's horse, he reached for the loose reins. Now his handcuffed hands were only a foot from the scabbard that held the sheriff's Winchester.

Meanwhile, Canton had gained his balance in the mud and was slogging forward. He looked up just in time to see Jackson's right hand touch the stock of the rifle. He could go for his own six-gun, but it was surely plugged with mud and might explode in his hand.

"Look out boys, he's going for it!" Canton shouted.

In an instant, Deputy Ed Lloyd had his Colt out and pointed at Jackson's head. The outlaw froze. Out of the corner of his eye he could see Lloyd's gun. His gaze then shifted to the Winchester. It was not even half out of the scabbard. If he drew it another inch he knew he was a dead man.

Later, as Canton was climbing back on his horse, Jackson said: "If I could have got that gun, I would have settled with you, anyway." No doubt you would have, thought Canton, but, as he would often repeat as he told of the incident in later years, "an inch of a miss is as good as a mile."

The rest of the trip was uneventful, and Teton Jackson was returned to Idaho where he was convicted of horse stealing and sent to the penitentiary. About a month after he was confined, Canton received a letter from him. He told the sheriff that considering the circumstances under which he had been captured, he felt that he had been treated well, and that he understood now that Canton was only doing his duty and he, Jackson, did not hold it against him. Then, as almost an afterthought, Jackson added that the state of Idaho did not furnish prisoners tobacco, and would Canton send him a dollar or two so he could buy some. The sheriff was touched by the letter, and he sent a $20 bill, with a short note expressing his regrets as to how things had worked out.

Not long after that, Jackson escaped. Had it not been for the letter, Canton would have been concerned, since Teton, just prior to his conviction, had sworn revenge on the lawman. But Canton's lack of concern was short-lived. On examining Jackson's cell, prison authorities found a list of names of a dozen men whom Teton vowed to kill on sight, "no matter where or when he met them." The first name on the list was Johnson County Sheriff Frank Canton.

But the outlaw never made good his threat. He and Frank Canton never again crossed paths.

TOM HORN, EXTERMINATOR

Between the day 14-year-old Tom Horn ran away from his father's farm in Scotland County, Missouri, and the day he died at the end of a rope twenty-nine years later, his trail covered much of the American West. But Tom Horn "the outlaw" belongs solely to Wyoming. To this day, in some parts of the state, to lay in wait to kill a man is to "Tom Horn" him. In Wyoming, Tom was known as the "exterminator," a title he often used himself and one he became quite proud of.

Horn's first trips through Wyoming were on the Union Pacific, as a Pinkerton detective out of Denver. It was the early 1890s, and his work occasionally involved pursuing train robbers, but mostly consisted of doing a "hobo act," posing as a tramp to catch conductors and brakemen taking favors to let passengers ride without a ticket. Tom liked chasing robbers, but he despised spying on railroad employees, so when he learned that several Wyoming cattle ranchers were looking for "stock detectives" to run down rustlers, he bade the Pinkerton agency farewell.

Life on the open range suited Tom better. Prior to his Pinkerton days he had been an army scout, and he was comfortable on the trail. He liked being free to come and go as he wished and being accountable to no one as long as he did his job.

Tom's first assignment with the cattlemen was with the Swan Land and Cattle Company north of Cheyenne on Chugwater Creek. Officially, Tom was hired to break broncs; unofficially he was to keep an eye out for rustlers, expecially among his fellow wranglers. He did his work well, and over the next decade he moved on to similar jobs with other cattlemen. But sometime during those ten years, Tom Horn stepped over the line that the law draws on such conduct. He became an exterminator.

Some say it happened gradually. After torturous weeks on the trail runing down a range thief, Horn would frequently see him turned loose by a sympathetic jury, many of whom would return to their homes that same night to suppers of pilfered beef. The story goes that Horn repeatedly pointed out to his cattle baron employers that justice might be better served if his prey never saw the inside of a courtroom. Eventually, Tom took it upon himself to prove his point. Quietly, among several of the cattlemen, he let it be known that for a price, say $300, he would lay a rustler out cold and stiff. And to prove that he had done the job, he would leave a small rock under the victim's head.

Several of the cattlemen saw the logic in Tom's proposal, and before long he collected $600 for the disposal of two rustlers who prowled the ranches east of Laramie on Horse Creek.

Word soon got around that Horn had done the job, but there were no witnesses, and moreover the two victims were disliked by nearly everyone in the area. After a brief investigation, the local sheriff dropped the matter. This willingness on the part of the law to look the other way encouraged Tom to expand his operation. He rode west into Sweetwater County and offered his special service to large ranchers there. Soon just his name brought fear even to the boldest cattle thief.

Tom's fame was due partly to his willingness to take credit for almost every dead body that turned up in his wake. How many of these victims were truly his will never be known, but he became the most feared killer in Wyoming. His name

Tom Horn, awaiting trial in the Laramie County jail in 1902. (*American Heritage Center, University of Wyoming*)

brought far more chills to the average settler than even the notorious Wild Bunch, who seldom bothered anyone except bank tellers and express car agents.

The story is told that during the late 1890s some small ranchers suspected of having fattened their herds with stolen stock would never leave for town without their wives and children beside them on the wagon. Others, it was said, laughed at their precautions, reminding them that if Tom Horn wanted them dead, being surrounded by family would not save them.

Horn terrorized Wyoming rustlers continually until 1898, when the outbreak of the Spanish American War kindled in him a new spirit of adventure. Off he went to Cuba where he served as a civilian mule train packer. He saw no action, but along with many of his comrades he came down with fever and returned within a year. His job with the cattlemen was waiting for him, and as soon as his health permitted he was on the trail of rustlers once more.

In 1901, Tom hooked up with a prominent cattleman near Laramie named John Coble. Although now too well known to operate under the cover of an ordinary cow puncher, Tom still frequently mingled with neighboring ranchers, always on the alert for anyone attempting to sample his employer's stock. While on his rounds for Coble, Horn became acquainted with a family named Miller who, at the time, were boarding an attractive school teacher. Tom kept pretty close contact with the Millers, not only because of the school marm, but also because the Millers, John Coble, and another ranching family in the area named Nickell had for years been involved in a strange three-sided feud.

Kels Nickell and his family had settled in the region first and, on the arrival of the Millers, launched a continuous haggle over range rights. Then along came the wealthy Coble, who was immediately accused of plotting to buy up all available land in an attempt to squeeze out the smaller ranchers.

The feud was fought both in the courts and on the trail. One day Nickell slashed Coble's belly open with a knife, and Coble had him arrested, only to see him get off with a plea of self-defense. Shortly thereafter Nickell took a slice out of Miller, who from that day on never left home without a shotgun on the wagon seat beside him. One day Miller's gun slipped off the seat, fell to the ground and discharged, killing one of his sons. Miller, blind with rage and grief, blamed Nickell for the boy's death and vowed that he would someday get even.

On a bright July morning in 1901, it appeared that he did. The body of one of Nickell's sons, 14-year-old Willie, was found on the road just outside the gate to his father's ranch, two gaping bullet holes in his chest. But suspicion soon shifted from Miller to Tom Horn when the sheriff released a statement that witnesses who saw the body reported that the boy had fallen on his face when shot, but it then appeared that someone had turned him over on his back and had carefully placed a small rock under his head.

Horn was questioned, but no arrest was made: the rock by itself, although known to be Horn's trademark, was not considered sufficient evidence that Tom had done the killing. Five months went by, and it appeared that the murder would go unsolved. Then, in December, Horn received an interesting letter from an old acquaintance, United States Deputy Marshal Joe LeFors of Cheyenne. According to LeFors, a group of Montana cattlemen were having trouble with rustlers and needed an experienced "stock detective" to chase them down. LeFors said if Tom was interested in the job, he would recommend him. Several more letters followed, and the two men arranged to meet at LeFors's office in Cheyenne in January.

It should have occurred to Horn that LeFors might have an ulterior motive in arranging the meeting. In fact, Tom's lady friend, the school teacher, had warned Tom to "look out for Joe LeFors, he is trying to find out something." But Horn attributed her concern to statements made by the Miller family, who bore a strong grudge against LeFors over some past encounter. Also, LeFors had no jurisdiction in the Nickell killing. Wyoming was now a state, and the crime was a local matter, with jurisdiction in the hands of county and state officials. In addition, it was not unusual that Joe LeFors would offer to arrange for Horn to hook up with cattlemen in another state. Lawmen frequently came up with such arrangements to persuade a troublemaker to move out of their jurisdiction. It was an acceptable, and face-saving, method of easing the burden of local law enforcement.

Thus, Tom's guard was down on that cold January day in 1902 when he strolled into LeFors's office in Cheyenne.

Wyoming peace officer, Joe LeFors, who engineered the arrest of Tom Horn. (*American Heritage Center, University of Wyoming*)

Moreover, it was said that Tom was carrying a belly-full of whiskey and that had he been sober, he may well have been suspicious of the marshal's curious preoccupation with the six-month-old Nickell killing. Horn wanted to talk about the offer in Montana, but LeFors kept steering the conversation back to the Nickell affair. Finally, perhaps with his mind fuzzy from too much alcohol, Tom must have concluded that LeFors was merely trying to satisfy himself that Tom had the talent and the hardness to handle a tough assignment. So when LeFors kept pestering him on how he accomplished the Willie Nickell murder without leaving a clue that could convict him, Tom responded with some very incriminating statements—statements he later claimed were made only because he was drunk and eager to brag.

But Tom's loose talk sealed his fate. LeFors had a deputy sheriff from Laramie County and a court stenographer hid-

National Guard troops patrolling downtown Cheyenne prior to the hanging of Tom Horn. There was speculation that an attempt might be made to free him at the last minute. (*American Heritage Center, University of Wyoming*)

den in the back room. Every word of the conversation was taken down and later used against Horn in court.

Students of outlaw history still disagree as to whether Horn actually killed the Nickell youth. A jury, however, said he did, although to this day Wyoming lawyers argue over whether he received a fair trial. By today's standards he certainly did not, and the jury's verdict would be overturned. But in 1903, after years of watching many Wyoming outlaws go lightly punished for their crimes, the public cried out for revenge. On September 30, 1903, the Supreme Court of Wyoming, in the longest opinion handed down in a criminal case, affirmed the jury's guilty verdict. And shortly thereafter, Tom Horn, the exterminator, was himself exterminated.

BUTCH CASSIDY AND THE WILD BUNCH

Probably the most likable outlaw that roamed Wyoming was Robert LeRoy Parker, alias Butch Cassidy. Although hardly the Robin Hood some of his fans have made him out to be, he was certainly not cut from the same cloth as most of his contemporaries. The average outlaw in his day was ignorant and mean; Cassidy was neither. He was bright and personable, and there is no evidence that he ever killed a man, except, perhaps, during the famous shootout with Bolivian soldiers that reportedly ended his career in 1909.

Except for the fact that Cassidy was indeed an outlaw, there have been few disparaging words said about him. Even wanted posters distributed by Pinkerton's National Detective Agency described him as the "cheerful and amiable" bandit. He was a handsome man; rugged, square-jawed, but with a pleasant, almost gentle face.

Butch Cassidy was born in Beaver, Utah, in 1866. His family were Mormons who had migrated to the West a decade earlier. Young Parker, then called Bob, was 13 when he had his first brush with the law. On a trip to town to buy a pair of trousers he found the store closed. Rather than make another trip, he quietly let himself in, picked out the pants he needed, and left a note that he would pay the next time he came to town. The storekeeper was not amused and complained to the sheriff.

Young Bob soon began resisting the strict religious training imposed on Mormon youth, and a few years after the store incident, he took up with a local drifter named Mike Cassidy, who occasionally supplemented his ranch hand's earnings with rustled steers. Mike Cassidy became the youth's hero and mentor, and before long the boy joined in on Mike's raids.

In the summer of 1884, a handful of steers carrying some of Bob's over-branding wandered back to their original herds. The owners put the law on Parker, and rather than bring shame to his family, the boy packed up and left,

Inner circle of the "Wild Bunch." Front row, left-to-right, Harry Longaaugh (The Sundance Kid), Ben Kilpatrick, and George Leroy Parker (Butch Cassidy). Back row, left-to-right, Will Carver and Harvey Logan. This portrait, reportedly taken as a joke, was made during the gang's assembly in Fort Worth, Texas in 1901. (*Denver Public Library, Western History Department.*)

adopting, as he did, the name of his former saddlemate.

Robert LeRoy Parker, now Butch Cassidy, headed east to the mines at Telluride, Colorado, where he got a job as a mule driver. Tiring of this, he struck out for Wyoming, where he drifted from ranch to ranch as a cowhand.

In 1889, Cassidy and a fellow drifter named Al Hainer bought a piece of land near Lander, where for a while they gave the appearance of homesteading. But soon they grew restless and returned once more to the range.

There is some evidence that Cassidy officially became an outlaw in June 1889, when he and a few friends rode back to Telluride and held up the San Miguel Valley Bank. Some believe, however, that his first major crime was two years earlier, when he and three brothers, the McCartys, tried to hold up a Denver & Rio Grande train 5 miles east of Grand

Junction, Colorado, on November 3, 1887. According to information from the Pinkerton files, Butch played only a minor role in this robbery, which was a flop, thanks to a stubborn express messenger who refused to open his safe. In the later bank robbery at Telluride, Butch and his comrades reportedly used relay teams of horses for their escape, a practice that became a specialty with Cassidy, and one picked up by other outlaws of the day.

Little was seen of Butch after the Telluride robbery until 1894, when a Fremont County deputy sheriff rode into Lander with him in tow. He had a gash in his head where a slug from the deputy's pistol had made a new part in his hair, and a bruise on his face in the shape of a gun barrel. The charge against him was stealing horses. He claimed that he was innocent, that he had only purchased the horses (but there is little doubt that he knew they were stolen). Two years later, on being released from prison at Laramie, Butch was bitter over what he considered an unjustice.

The story goes that Cassidy more or less bargained for his release. According to Butch, the governor of Wyoming offered him a pardon if he would "go straight." Butch said he told the governor that "there was no use promising to go different. I was already in too deep. But I said I would promise not to worry Wyoming if he'd pardon me out."

Once out, Cassidy wasted no time in putting together a new gang. It would eventually be known as the "Wild Bunch," a name taken from the gang that rode with the Daltons down in Oklahoma. Among the early joiners was Harry Longabaugh, the Sundance Kid, who had recently been opening express cars on the Great Northern Railroad in Montana. Other gang members were picked up from among the residents of the Hole-in-the-Wall in Johnson County.

The new outfit's first major crime may have been a bank holdup in central Utah in early 1896, but there is little record of this robbery. Another bank robbery, at Montpelier, Idaho, in August 1896, is generally accepted as the first by the Wild Bunch in which Cassidy participated.

The gang may have been busy with minor holdups during the next two years, but if so, they are lost to history. Cassidy himself was connected with a robbery of the Pleasant Valley Coal Company at Castle Gate, Utah, in April 1897. Up to this point it appeared that he was keeping his promise to the governor of Wyoming not to commit any crimes in his state.

Except for the Castle Gate affair, Cassidy and the Wild Bunch have not been tied to any major crimes during 1896-98, yet they apparently were blamed for most of the mischief that occurred in the Rocky Mountain states during that period. There is an account of a meeting of the governors of the states of Colorado, Utah, and Wyoming in March 1898, in which they agreed to handpick a select squad of law officers from each state to go after the Wild Bunch and exterminate them. But on the announcement of the war with Spain, the plan was called off.

Cassidy's promise may have been broken in April 1899 with the robbery of an express car on the Union Pacific at Wilcox, Wyoming. (Some say that Butch may have helped plan it but did not participate in it.) The robbery could be considered a success, since the gang garnered about $50,000, but otherwise it marked the beginning of the end of the Wild Bunch. A hastily organized posse hardly let the outlaws get out of sight. In an ensuing gunfight, a local sheriff was killed, and possibly one of the gang, who was buried by his comrades in the hills behind a friend's ranch on the road between Casper and Lander.

Despite the combined efforts of Union Pacific detectives, local authorities, the state militia, and a pack of howling bloodhounds, the gang eventually eluded their pursuers. Cassidy headed north into Montana, where he hitched a ride on a train bound for Seattle. From there he caught another train to Los Angeles, where he closeted himself away in a seedy sailor's hotel.

Other members of the gang were not so lucky. Harvey Logan and Bob Lee left a trail of stolen bank notes. The Pinkertons traced them to Harvey's brother, Lonnie Logan, and arrested him. Lee showed up and was also arrested, but

Harvey (Kid Curry) Logan, member of the Wild Bunch and one of Wyoming's most feared train robbers. *(Union Pacific Railroad Museum)*

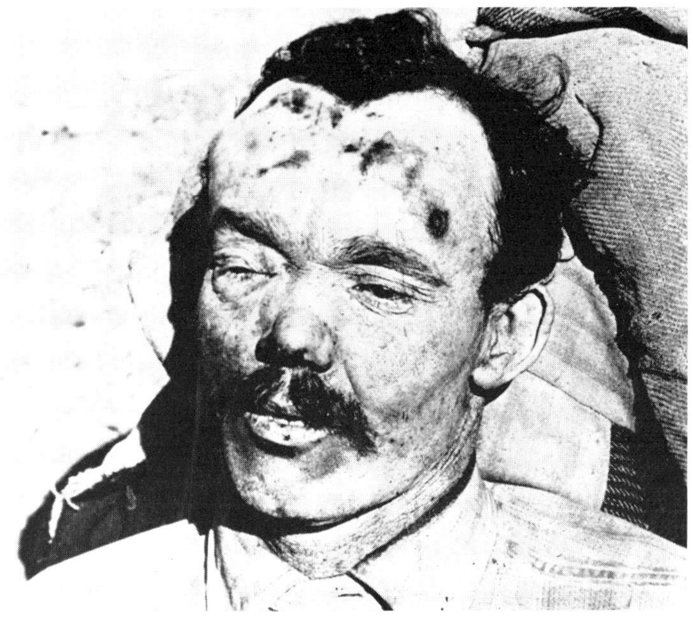

"Flat Nose" George Currie, likable member of the Wild Bunch. This photograph was taken in April 1900 shortly after Currie was killed by a posse who took him for a rustler they were pursuing. (*Pinkerton's, Inc.*)

Harvey Logan got away. Two months later, a third member of the bunch, "Flat Nose" George Currie, was killed by a Utah sheriff who mistook him for a rustler.

There is an interesting story that in early 1900 Butch decided to give up his life of crime and request a pardon. Through a lawyer he made contact with the governor of Utah, Heber Wells, and promised to go straight if he were forgiven for his past misdeeds. The plea was useless, because Cassidy was wanted in Wyoming as well, where Utah officials had no jurisdiction. The Utah governor did suggest an alternative plan, however. If Cassidy would ask the Union Pacific Railroad to drop its charges against him in return for his promise to go straight, the governor would do what he could to persuade the railroad to accept the proposal. And to make the deal attractive, Wells suggested that Cassidy offer to become a railway express guard. This would allow the railroad to keep an eye on him and, it was hoped, persuade other bandits to stay clear of the Union Pacific.

As preposterous as the plan was, the railroad officials agreed to meet with Cassidy and talk. A time and place were set. Butch showed up, but the Union Pacific officials were delayed en route, and Butch, suspecting a double cross, gave up and left.

Cassidy was through trying to make deals, and a patched-up Wild Bunch was ready to rob trains again. The gang struck the Union Pacific at Tipton, Wyoming, on August 29, 1900. The robbery was a repeat of the Wilcox affair, except this time the getaway was clean. The railroad reported a loss of only $54, but other sources place the haul closer to $50,000, some of which Cassidy may have buried near Huntington, Nevada.

Butch drifted about until the spring of 1901. In June, he and Harvey Logan put together a makeshift crew and on July 3 staged a midday holdup of the Great Northern Coast Flyer at Exeter Switch, near Wagner, Montana. The robbery went off without a hitch and the gang netted $40,000.

After nearly a decade of robbing trains and banks to-

Railroad posse that chased the Wild Bunch and other Wyoming train robbers at the turn of the century. (*Union Pacific Railroad Museum*)

gether, Cassidy and Harry Longabaugh had become close friends. And by 1901, they had finally achieved the goal of the western outlaw, a stake large enough to "head south." For most outlaws, "south" was across the border into Mexico, but for Cassidy and Longabaugh it was South America. Sometime in 1901 the two outlaws, together with Longabaugh's girl friend, Etta Place, sailed for Argentina, where they became partners on a cattle and sheep ranch in the province of Chubut.

The trio led an idyllic life for three years, until 1904, when Cassidy may have been recognized by local authorities. Perhaps using this as an excuse, the two fugitives resumed their criminal ways, robbing banks in Argentina and Bolivia and possibly introducing train robbery to the area.

Several people say they saw Butch back in the United States in 1908. In February of that year, he was believed to have written a letter to his employer at the time, C. R. Glass, manager of a tin mine. But there Cassidy's trail ended; nothing more was heard for over twenty years.

In 1930, an article on Cassidy appeared in the April issue

of *Elks Magazine*. The author, western writer Arthur Chapman, claimed he had obtained new information about Cassidy from an American mining engineer named Percy Seibert who had worked with the outlaw in 1908. According to Seibert, both Cassidy and Harry Longabaugh were killed in a blazing gun battle with Bolivian soldiers at San Vincente sometime in 1909. Since there was no apparent reason to doubt the story, and since nothing had been heard from either Cassidy or Longabaugh for over two decades, the story was accepted by most writers and western historians. The file was closed on the two fugitives.

But the file remained closed for only six years. In July 1936, word filtered out of Lander, Wyoming, that Butch Cassidy had been seen there the previous year. The story would have caused little interest except that there were still a handful of residents living in Lander who had known Butch in the old days. On being interviewed, one of these old-timers admitted that he had indeed seen Butch, who had told him that he was living in Seattle, Washington, under the name Bill Phillips. This intrigued several Wyoming historians, who decided to dig deeper. Unfortunately, they spent too much time gathering more information in and around Lander and did not send somebody directly to Seattle to check on Mr. Phillips. When word finally came that there was indeed a William Phillips in Seattle, it was found that he had died of cancer on July 20, 1937.

Was this William Phillips really Butch Cassidy? The evidence is strong that he was. A Montana writer, Larry Pointer, devoted countless hours to settling the question. The results of his efforts, a book entitled *In Search of Butch Cassidy*, is a superb account of the outlaw's life. In his research, Pointer uncovered a fascinating manuscript said to have been written by the deceased Mr. Phillips himself. It was entitled, "The Bandit Invincible, the Story of Butch Cassidy." After an exhaustive study, Pointer concluded that the manuscript was genuine and that Phillips and Cassidy were one and the same. Although childishly written, occasionally vague, and obviously self-serving, "The Bandit Invincible," Pointer feels, contained information only Butch would have known.

Cassidy's sister, Mrs. Lula Parker Betenson of Utah, who wrote her own book about her famous brother, could have settled the matter, but chose not to. She did admit, however, that Butch did not die in Bolivia, that he had returned to this country, and that he had settled in "the Northwest." She said he lived until 1937.

THE NOTORIOUS ED TRAFTON

Closely following Teton Jackson as Jackson Hole's most famous home-grown outlaw was an outrageous character named Ed Harrington, alias Ed Trafton. Trafton's fame was fleeting, and he never will be listed among the frontier's most successful badmen. In fact, things just never seemed to work out too well for Ed. He always seemed to set his sights a little too high, and luck was seldom on his side.

Trafton's story begins sometime in the 1880s, when he first showed up in Jackson Hole. It is believed that he came from the East; just where is not certain, possibly Missouri, since it was often said that as a boy his heroes were Jesse and Frank James and that his life's ambition was someday to be as famous. He almost made it—but not quite.

In the beginning, Trafton differed little from the dozens of settlers in the valley along the Snake River, except perhaps for a persistent rumor that he had a history of minor infractions of the law. This was soon confirmed when his neighbors began to notice that he had a penchant for borrowing other people's horses without their knowledge.

Within a year, Trafton and two partners, Jim Robertson and Lum Nickerson, were knee deep in an active horse-stealing business, an operation that flourished until May 1889, when a local posse burst into their cabin hideout on the Teton River, arrested Nickerson, and shot Robertson dead. Trafton was smart enough to be elsewhere at the time, but when he got word about his partners, he unwisely chose to gather up some quick money for a getaway by robbing a general store at Rexburg. He was promptly arrested and hauled off to jail.

Jails were not exactly plentiful in the Teton wilderness in those days, and Ed soon found himself in a cell with his partner, Lum Nickerson. This was a fortunate break for Ed, because Lum's wife, on her second visit to see her husband, smuggled in a pistol. Ed took charge, and in minutes he and Nickerson were on their way out of town.

But the two horse thieves' stint at freedom was brief. On their second day out a posse found them standing helplessly before the swollen Snake River, too frightened to try to swim across. They were taken back to jail, and Trafton eventually stood trial, collecting a sentence of twenty-five years in the territorial penitentiary. But again fate smiled on Ed. His devoted mother came into a large insurance settlement from the death of a relative, and through the use of the money and her tireless effort, Ed was pardoned after four years.

Trafton returned to the valley a changed and repentant man. Jackson Hole residents were not the kind to hold a person forever guilty of past deeds, and Ed was soon welcomed back into the fold. Furthermore, Ed, who could be a charmer when necessary, so thoroughly convinced local authorities that he had turned over a new leaf that he was offered a contract with the government to carry mail in and out of the little hamlet of Pierre's Hole. The work did not pay much, but it got Ed acquainted with several important persons in the valley, one of whom was the noted novelist Owen Wister, at the time gathering material for his famous novel, *The Virginian.* Trafton would later claim that Wister had so enjoyed his friendship that he used him as a model for his hero in the book. Those who knew the real Trafton, however, would argue that if Ed was used for a character in the novel, it was for Trampus, the villain.

After a while Trafton became bored with his mailman's work and drifted away into other ventures, most probably dishonest. Little was heard from him again around Jackson

Hole until one morning in July 1914, when, beside a winding, rocky trail in Yellowstone National Park, he and a confederate named Charles Erpenbach held up fifteen stagecoaches in less than an hour.

Trafton was not the first to eye the Yellowstone stage route. Park regulations prohibited visitors from carrying firearms, which made them attractive targets for bandits. The last holdup of a stagecoach, however, had occurred in 1908, and Ed Trafton felt it was time for another.

The Yellowstone Naional Park stage lines ran tourist stagecoaches through the park at intervals of from one to five minutes, with the average coach carrying five or six passengers. Ed chose for his assault a site near Shoshone Point, between Old Faithful Inn and the Thumb Lunch Station. As the first stage of the morning slowed for the point, Trafton, his face hidden by a flowered bandana and his hat pulled low over his brow, stepped from behind a giant boulder and shouted to the driver to pull his team to a halt. It was 10:00 a.m., hardly an hour for a holdup, but when the driver spotted Ed's menacing Winchester, he realized immediately the stranger meant business.

Warning the passengers that they had better behave because he had a helper stationed nearby with another rifle, Trafton ordered them out of the stage and made them line up before him in single file. One by one they passed by and dropped their valuables in a sack. Smugly, with the confident air of a highwayman of old, Ed watched as the passengers emptied their pockets. When they had finished, he ordered them back into the coach and told the driver to pull on around the point and down the trail a piece, reminding him again that he was under the constant observation of his partner, and if he tried to escape he would promptly be shot off his seat.

One by one, as the succeeding stages reached the point, Trafton ordered the drivers to halt, and the scene was repeated. As soon as the passengers were relieved of their cash and jewelry, the drivers were ordered to pull ahead and line up behind the others. The driver of the lead stage, still frozen to his seat by the thought of a rifle slug splitting his shoulder blades, had not budged an inch.

When the sixteenth stage failed to show up, Trafton figured he had pushed his luck far enough. For their hours' work, Ed and his confederate had collected just over $1,000. But for some of their victims, especially those who had wisely carried only a few dollars on them, the experience was well worth the price. They had come west to enjoy the frontier at its lusty best, and they could now return to tell their friends of a first-hand encounter with a real western bandit.

As the last of the passengers lined up to contribute, an elderly lady, shabbily dressed and obviously on a trip west for which she had saved a lifetime, dropped her purse as she approached Trafton's sack. Ed picked it up and handed it back, saying "Here madam, you keep this. You look as if you need it more than I do."

A few grins began to appear on the faces of the passengers patiently waiting in the stages stacked up ahead, the line now so long that the nearest coach was only a dozen or so yards from Trafton and his last victims. As menacing as Trafton had appeared in the beginning, many of the passengers now began to see him in a different light—perhaps more actor than outlaw. Undoubtedly, many believed that it was all an act to entertain guests of the park, and that their money would soon be returned. Several in the crowd carried cameras, and somebody shouted "Hey, how about some pictures." Trafton thought for a second, then adjusted his bandana and hat, and replied, "Sure, why not."

The robbery made nation's headlines. In New York, an editor for the *Times* wryly commented that if the bandits had really been on their toes, they would have had a Hollywood camera crew standing by. "Instead of leaving its immortalization to amateur snapshooters, the robbers should have arranged with expert makers of moving pictures for an adequate—and profitable—reproduction of a romantic and interesting happening, pleasantly reminiscent of the good old days when highway robbery was in its prime."

Park officials and local scouts combed the area for signs of the robbers' getaway route. About a half mile south of Shoshone Point they picked up the trail of two horses, leading due south and out of the park toward Jackson Hole. About the same time they found another set of tracks, this time a lone man on foot. These led in a southwesterly direction, toward a cabin on Conant Creek inhabited by a local character named Charles Erpenbach.

Erpenbach was arrested and charged with taking part in the robbery. Eventually he confessed and named Trafton as his accomplice. Ed was arrested by federal officers at Rupert, Idaho on May 22, 1915, and six months later was convicted and sentenced to five years at Leavenworth penitentiary.

But even a second stretch in prison taught the incorrigible Trafton nothing. When he was finally released he once again drifted from one outrageous scheme to another, the most outlandish being a plot to build an armored car and use it to kidnap the president of the Mormon church. When this fell through (word leaked out while Ed was still building the car), he wandered out to Hollywood to try to sell the story of his life to the studios. There were no takers, and it is believed that he ended up playing a few bit parts in western movies.

Although it has not been verified, there is a story that it all came to an end one day in the late 1920s in a soda fountain in downtown Hollywood. Ed was sitting on a stool having a cool drink when, suddenly and without a sound he slumped over, lay his head down on the counter, and quietly passed away from heart failure. An unglamorous end to one of Wyoming's most colorful outlaws.

BILL CARLISLE, LONE BANDIT

Back in the early 1950s, motorists traveling through southwestern Wyoming who happened to stop at a little cafe and gas station just outside of Kemmerer, where U.S. 30

Union Pacific depot at Green River where Will Carlisle boarded the Portland Rose to become the last of Wyoming's famous train robbers. (*Wyoming State Archives, Museums and Historical Department*)

crosses U.S. 189, probably paid little attention to the proprietor. He was ordinary looking, in his late fifties, with moderately rugged features, and just a slight trace of a twinkle in his eyes. It was that twinkle that should have suggested that maybe this individual was somebody special, different perhaps from the hundreds of other hardy residents who populated this harsh mountain region.

This man was indeed special. Behind that twinkle lay a story that would have kept a traveler spellbound for hours. The man was Bill Carlisle, last of Wyoming's notorious train robbers.

Bill's story began on a cold night in February 1916. The town of Green River was in the early stages of a typical Wyoming blizzard. At the snow-covered Union Pacific depot, the eastbound Portland Rose was just about to pull out into the frozen winter darkness. As the wheels of the observation car began to turn, a shadowy figure reached into the collar of his heavy mackinaw and pulled a white scarf up over his face. Then quickly he leaped on board and stepped into the car.

It was near midnight, and most of the passengers had retired to their berths. A lone woman sat reading under a bright wall lamp. When the door opened she looked up and gasped as she saw a gun in the intruder's hand. "Calm down lady," he said, "no harm will come to you if you keep quiet."

The next car to the front was a sleeper, and just inside was a porter, carefully running down his list of passengers to see if they had everything they needed for the night. Pointing his gun at the bright shiny buttons on the porter's starched uniform, the masked man ordered the porter to march in front of him down the aisle, from berth to berth, and collect all the money and valuables from the male passengers. "But don't open any berths occupied by women and children," he said.

The porter did as he was told, and when they had finished with the last berth, the intruder slipped out the door. Thinking the robber had jumped off the platform between the cars, the porter pulled the bell cord for the train to stop. But the masked man had climbed the sleeper's narrow ladder to the top of the car. When the train pulled to a stop, he jumped off the opposite side and vanished in the darkness.

The following morning stunned Union Pacific officials converged on the scene. It had been years since a U.P. train had been robbed, and a successful holdup by a lone bandit was practically unheard of, even in the old days. "Fool's luck," the railroad officials insisted. "It could never happen again."

They were wrong. On April 5, the man in the white mask struck again. This time it was the U.P.'s crack Overland Limited a few miles west of Cheyenne. Again the robber was alone, and again he was successful. As the passengers stared in disbelief, the bandit proudly boasted that he was the robber who had held up the Portland Rose near Green River, and that there was a $1,500 reward on his head. "If anyone wants it, now is a good time to get it," he challenged. No one took him up on it. As before, the bandit ordered a porter to pass his cap, and the male passengers obediently dropped in their money.

The robber's daring delighted the press, and the "man in the white mask" became an instant celebrity. In the fifty-year history of western train robberies, only a handful of bandits had ever tried to rob a passenger coach or sleeper single-handedly, and few had succeeded. This man had beaten the odds soundly and was thoroughly enjoying the game.

As with most well-publicized crimes, law enforcement agencies and newspaper offices were flooded with tips as to the robber's whereabouts. Most were checked out and proved false. Shortly after the second robbery, however, the *Denver Post* received an anonymous letter from a man who said he was the bandit. To prove it, the writer said, "I am enclosing a watch chain I took in that last holdup." Enclosed, indeed, was a watch chain taken from a passenger on the Overland Limited.

Apparently the writer was concerned about several arrests made of known criminals who happened to have no alibi for the nights of the two robberies. "To convince the officers they have the wrong men in jail," the writer added, "I will hold up the next Union Pacific train west of Laramie." The authorities refused to believe the writer's boast, insisting instead that if the writer were the bandit, he was trying to create a diversion and would strike another train.

But the bandit was true to his word. The next train west of Laramie was Union Pacific Limited No. 21. As it pulled out of Hanna, a small station between Rawlins and Medicine Bow, a man standing next to a railroad guard suddenly slipped on a white mask. The guard could not believe his eyes. Humiliated, with a gun pointed at his head, he was forced to march down the aisle, taking up a collection of cash and valuables in his cap.

This time, however, luck was not with the robber. As he leaped off the train he severely wrenched his ankle. Barely able to hobble, he could cover very little ground. Dawn found him hiding in the willowed bottoms along the North Platte River, with a hastily formed posse breathing down his

Will Carlisle, in handcuffs, following his arrest for train robbery in Sweetwater County. (*Wyoming State Archives, Museums and Historical Department*)

neck. Hidden in the heavy brush, he was not spotted by the possemen until they were almost upon him. He easily could have killed several, but he chose not to make a fight of it. This so impressed a reporter who had come along on the chase that he used it as the lead for his story. The next day the *Denver Post* carried the following headline: "Bandit Surrenders Rather Than Turn Killer—Lays Down His Guns When Officers Are Afraid to Disarm Him."

Back in Denver, the bandit's flair for the dramatic had already cost him his anonymity. The *Post* reproduced his letter on the front page, and a rancher near Cheyenne recognized the handwriting as that of a former wrangler named Bill Carlisle.

Delighted over the publicity he was receiving, the man in the white mask turned out to be a most affable prisoner. His background, if true, painted an interesting portrait of a train robber. Born in York, Pennsylvania, near a railroad yard, he had spent much of his childhood with boyhood gangs playing Jesse James in abandoned coaches. As did all the boys from his neighborhood, he consistently snitched coal from the tracks, and the railroad "bulls" were forever chasing him. At 13, he hopped a freight and spent a summer dodging brakemen and railroad "dicks" whom he considered among the most "cruel and ruthless" individuals he ever met. To add to his dislike of railroads, his oldest brother, a locomotive engineer, was killed in a wreck. When questioned about his first robbery, Carlisle gave this story:

> I held up that first train because I was desperate. Hungry, cold, jobless, with only a nickel in my pocket . . . while I was standing at the station waiting to jump a freight, the Overland Limited came through. I stood looking at the warm, comfortable coaches with their bright lights and well-dressed people . . . The idea of holding up the train came to me on the spur of the moment. That train pulled out but while I was still wondering what to do, another passenger pulled in—and I got on.

Carlisle was swiftly convicted of the robberies and sentenced to the Wyoming State Penitentiary for life. It was a harsh penalty, even for armed robbery. Once behind the walls, however, Bill became a model prisoner, never complaining and seldom mixing with the more troublesome, hard-nosed inmates. At the end of three years, the board of pardons reduced his sentence to fifty years.

Bill should have been thankful, but fifty years was still a long time, and one cold November night he climbed inside a packing crate in the prison shirt factory and had himself delivered to the local freight house with a shipment bound for Chicago. A week later he was back robbing the Union Pacific.

But Bill's first choice on his return to train robbery was a bad one. It was November 21, 1919, and the coaches still occasionally carried doughboys on their way home from the war front. Bill picked such a coach. He was inside with his gun out before he realized his error. Momentarily confused, he finally passed his hat among the few civilians present, telling the soldiers to "keep your money, boys, I don't want it."

When the train slowed for Medicine Bow, Carlisle dashed for the vestibule to leap off. But just as he stepped through the door, one of the train guards jumped him. Bill's gun discharged, and a bullet ripped through his hand and wrist. Once on the ground, he raced for cover behind a line of sheep corrals that bordered the tracks. The disorganized soldiers were slow pouring out of the coach, and Carlisle scrambled across the frozen prairie out of sight.

Weak from his wound, he was forced to seek help from local residents. As a result, the law was soon close behind. He was eventually cornered in a miner's cabin above Estabrook, a mountain resort. The posse came while Bill was having breakfast. On hearing the horses, he stepped to the doorway of the cabin, coatless, vest open, hands empty. The jittery sheriff, however, took no chances. "Hands up!" he shouted. But Bill's wounded right arm, now stiff all the way to the shoulder, refused to budge. Thinking that Carlisle was going for his gun, the sheriff raised his rifle and fired. The bullet smashed into Bill's chest.

Carlisle lived, but his recovery was slow. When his health did return, he became a changed man. He enrolled in a business course by mail, learned to use a typewriter, and became the prison librarian. By the time he was eligible for parole, he had so impressed the prison chaplain, a Catholic priest named Father Schellinger, that he guaranteed Bill's return to honest life. "Should Bill Carlisle ever commit another crime," Father Schellinger informed the prison officials, "I will serve time either for him or with him."

With the priest's help, Carlisle was finally released. He had been behind bars for twenty years, but he was ready to start a new life. Father Schellinger arranged for him to borrow money, and he opened a cigar store in the town of Kemmerer. Later, he bought the gas station and cafe.

Years later, when asked why he had returned to the very area where he was once known as a notorious train robber, Bill replied, "The best place to find a thing is where you lost it."

BIBLIOGRAPHY

Beal, Merrill D. *The Story of Man in Yellowstone.* Caldwell, Idaho: The Caxton Printers, 1949.

Betts, Robert B. *Along the Ramparts of the Tetons: The Saga of Jackson Hole, Wyoming.* Boulder: Colorado Associated University Press, 1978.

Breihan, Carl W. *The Escapades of Frank and Jesse James.* New York: Frederick Fell Publishers, 1974.

Burt, Struthers. *Powder River: Let 'er Buck.* New York: Farrar & Rinehart, 1938.

Canton, Frank M. *Frontier Trails: The Autobiography of Frank M. Canton.* Boston: Houghton Mifflin Company, 1930.

Condit, Thelma Gatchell. "The Hole in the Wall." *Annals of Wyoming,* Vol. 28, April 1956, pp. 28-40; Vol. 30, April 1958, pp. 17-35; Vol. 31, April 1959, pp. 53-75.

Coutant, C. G., "Thomas Jefferson Carr: A Frontier Sheriff." *Annals of Wyoming,* Vol. 20, July 1948, pp. 156-176.

Haynes, Jack Ellis. "Yellowstone Stage Holdups." *1952 Denver Westerners Brandbook.* Denver: University of Denver Press, 1952.

Horan, James D. *Desperate Men.* New York: G. P. Putnam's Sons, 1949.

Howe, Elvon L., ed. *Rocky Mountain Empire.* Garden City, N.Y.: Doubleday & Company, 1946.

Larson, T. A. *History of Wyoming.* Lincoln: University of Nebraska Press, 1978.

Mercer, A. S. *The Banditti of the Plains.* Reprint. Norman: University of Oklahoma Press, 1953.

Monaghan, Jay. *The legend of Tom Horn: Last of the Bad Men.* Indianapolis: Bobbs Merrill Company, 1946.

Paine, Lauran. *Tom Horn: Man of the West.* Barre, Mass.: Barre Publishing Company, 1963.

Patterson, Richard. *Train Robbery: The Birth, Flowering and Decline of a Notorious Western Enterprise.* Boulder, Colo.: Johnson Books, 1981.

Pence, MaryLou and Homsher, Lola M. *The Ghost Towns of Wyoming*. New York: Hastings House, 1956.

Pointer, Larry. *In Search of Butch Cassidy*. Norman: University of Oklahoma Press, 1977.

Sandborn, Margaret. *The Grand Tetons: The Story of the Men Who Tamed the Western Wilderness*. New York: G. P. Putnam's Sons, 1978.

Acknowledgments

No book, even a small one, can be written without the help of many people. For their research efforts, the author wishes to thank the staff at the University of Wyoming Division of Rare Books and Special Collections at Laramie, and the Wyoming State Archives, Museums and Historical Department, Cheyenne. Thanks go also to Wyoming historian Jim Laird of Cheyenne, for his critical, yet welcome, comments. Last but not least, thanks to Michael McNierney, Editorial Director of Johnson Books, Boulder, Colorado, who saw the need to help preserve some of Wyoming's most interesting past, and to Leslie Burger, also of Johnson Books, for her expert editorial assistance.

R.P.